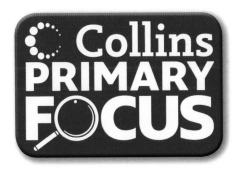

Vocabulary

Pupil Book 3

Louis Fidge and Sarah Lindsay

William Collins' dream of knowledge for all began with the publication of his first book in 1819. A self-educated mill worker, he not only enriched millions of lives, but also founded a flourishing publishing house. Today, staying true to this spirit, Collins books are packed with inspiration, innovation and practical expertise. They place you at the centre of a world of possibility and give you exactly what you need to explore it.

Collins. Freedom to teach.

Acknowledgements
p20, top: Eric Isselée/iStockphoto; p20, centre: Stephen Strathdee/iStockphoto; p20, bottom: Tempura/iStockphoto; p21, top: Peter Zurek/iStockphoto; p21, centre: Peter Zurek/iStockphoto; p21, bottom: haveseen/Shutterstock.

Published by Collins
An imprint of HarperCollins*Publishers* Ltd.
1 London Bridge Street
London
SE1 9GF

**Browse the complete Collins catalogue at
www.collinseducation.com**

Text © Louis Fidge and Sarah Lindsay 2013
Design and illustrations © HarperCollins*Publishers* Limited 2013

Previously published as *Collins Primary Word Work*, first published 1998; and *Collins Focus on Word Work*, first published 2002.

10 9 8 7 6 5 4 3

ISBN: 978-0-00-750102-1

Louis Fidge and Sarah Lindsay assert their moral right to be identified as the authors of this work.

British Library Cataloguing in Publication Data
A Catalogue record for this publication is available from the British Library.

Cover template: Laing & Carroll
Cover illustration: Paul McCaffrey
Series design: Neil Adams
Picture research: Gill Metcalfe
Illustrations: Stephanie Dix and Sue Woollatt.
Some illustrations have been used from the previous edition (978-0-00-713228-7).

Printed and bound in China.

MIX
Paper from
responsible sources
FSC www.fsc.org **FSC™ C007454**

FSC™ is a non-profit international organisation established to promote the responsible management of the world's forests. Products carrying the FSC label are independently certified to assure consumers that they come from forests that are managed to meet the social, economic and ecological needs of present and future generations, and other controlled sources.

Find out more about HarperCollins and the environment at
www.harpercollins.co.uk/green

Contents

Synonyms are words with **similar meanings**. We need to choose the **most appropriate** word that **best expresses** what we're trying to say.

Remember to use a thesaurus when looking for synonyms.

The words in bold are all synonyms for **angry**, but they all have a **slightly different meaning**.

I like to keep the books tidy. I get **irritated** when someone leaves them in a mess.

I thought Anna was my best friend. I was **upset** when she didn't invite me to her party.

I was **cross** when I was deliberately fouled just as I was about to score.

The man was **furious** when someone crashed into his new car.

Practice

Match each word in Set A with its synonym in Set B. Write down each pair.

Set A

new	wander	aid	broad	start
cunning	feeble	copy	strong	slim

Set B

weak	help	wide	sly	roam
imitate	powerful	modern	slender	begin

More to think about

Find the three words with similar meanings in each set.
Write down these synonyms.

1. brave   adult   fearless   attractive   courageous
2. snap   tell   inform   notice   notify
3. rough   harsh   argue   alarm   uneven
4. old   jolly   ancient   valuable   antique
5. special   remote   lonely   selfish   isolated

Now try these

1. Copy the sentences. Choose the best synonym from the box to complete each sentence.

   a)
snatched	seized	captured

   The police _____ the thief who had escaped.

   The mugger _____ the old lady's handbag.

   The eagle _____ the mouse in its claws.

   b)
adjust	change	alter

   My trousers were too long so my mum had to _____ them.

   A chameleon can _____ its colour to match its surroundings.

   You can usually _____ the colour on a TV set with its remote control.

2. Write sentences to show you know the difference in meaning between the three synonyms in each set.

   a) gobble   nibble   devour   b) pour   spill   drip

   c) kind   helpful   generous   d) examine   notice   recognise

Shortening words

We sometimes **shorten** words in different ways: by **leaving out letters**, by **leaving off suffixes or prefixes**, or by using **abbreviations**.

Leaving out letters:
ca**nn**ot = can't
ten of the clock = ten o'clock

It can't be ten o'clock already!

Leaving off suffixes or prefixes:
omni**bus** = bus
mathematics = maths

Shall we go for a bus ride or do our maths?

Using abbreviations:
Member of Parliament = MP

She's an important MP.

Practice

1. Match the contractions in Set A with their longer forms in Set B.

Set A

isn't   she's   I've   you'll   they'd   I'm   don't   we're   who's   it's

o'clock   shan't   Hallowe'en   how's   where've

Set B

I have   they would   it is   we are   I am   she is   you will   who is   do not

is not   shall not   where have   of the clock   how is   All Hallows Eve

2. Now underline the letter or letters that have been left out in each phrase.

More to think about

Write these sentences using the shorter form of the underlined words from the box.

> cycle   fridge   phone   rhino   photo   exam   hippo   miss   pram   zoo

1. The lady took a <u>photograph</u> of the baby in the <u>perambulator</u>.
2. The <u>telephone</u> rang while I was getting a drink from the <u>refrigerator</u>.
3. <u>Mistress</u> Smith said I did well in the <u>examination</u>.
4. Which is bigger – a <u>hippopotamus</u> or a <u>rhinoceros</u>?
5. I went on my <u>bicycle</u> to visit the <u>zoological gardens</u>.

Now try these

Rewrite these sentences using the correct abbreviations from the box.

> USA   UN   CD   MP   Dr   km/h   CID   v   JP

1. I saw the Arsenal <u>versus</u> Chelsea football match.
2. He drove the car at well over 80 <u>kilometres per hour</u>.
3. <u>Doctor</u> Jones comes from the <u>United States of America</u>.
4. The purpose of the <u>United Nations</u> is to safeguard world peace.
5. I bought a <u>compact disc</u> by my favourite band.
6. Mrs Currie used to be a <u>Justice of the Peace</u> but now she's been elected as our <u>Member of Parliament</u>.
7. The detective was from the <u>Criminal Investigation Department</u>.

Dialogue words and adverbs

Dialogue words are verbs that express the way we **say** things, like **said**, **replied**, **shouted**.

Adverbs are words that tell us **more about verbs**. Adverbs often tell us **how** something is done.

"Where did you get it?" she asked **accusingly**.

"Where did you get it?" she gasped **admiringly**.

"Where did you get it?" she laughed **scornfully**.

"Where did you get it?" she exclaimed **gratefully**.

Practice

Copy the sentences. Choose the best adverb to complete each sentence.

1. We shout _____ (loudly/fondly).

2. We laugh _____ (sadly/happily).

3. We whisper _____ (bravely/quietly).

4. We weep _____ (sadly/simply).

5. We answer _____ (kindly/correctly).

6. We argue _____ (quietly/noisily).

7. We sing _____ (tunefully/painfully).

More to think about

Copy the sentences. Choose a suitable adverb from the box to complete each one.

breathlessly	fondly	angrily	hopefully
sleepily	haltingly	honestly	fiercely

1. "It's nearly three in the morning," Tom yawned _____.

2. "You're a good daughter," Ann's mother said _____.

3. "Get away from me," the man snarled _____.

4. "I've run all the way home," gasped Sam _____.

5. "It's a g...g...g...ghost!" Tom stammered _____.

6. "Please may I come?" the child asked _____.

7. "I didn't do it," the suspect declared _____.

8. "That vacuum cleaner you sold me is rubbish!" complained the lady _____.

Now try these

Think of an adverb that you could use with each of these dialogue words to make them more interesting.

1. You can sigh _____.

2. You can chuckle _____.

3. You can grumble _____.

4. You can mutter _____.

5. You can yell _____.

6. You can explain _____.

7. You can insist _____.

8. You can ask _____.

Please

Sometimes we can group words according to their **roots** (origins).

The words can often be identified as they have the **same word** (or part of the word) **in common**.

Signum is the Latin word for a **sign**. Look at some of the words that come from it.

What do you notice about the sound of the **g** in the words?

Signify
design resign
Sign Signature
Signal

Practice

Copy these words. Write the root word that each one comes from.

1. disappearance
2. colouring
3. pressure
4. direction
5. helpful
6. continued
7. increased
8. likely
9. washing
10. recovery
11. attractive
12. television

Harbour   Beach

More to think about

Find and match a word from each of the three sets that share the same root word. Write down each matching set.

Set A

| detect | format | special | vary | statue |
| graph | telescope | cap | fact | medic |

Set B

| medical | factory | perform | capital | various |
| especially | detective | graphics | television | statement |

Set C

| captain | medicine | estate | speciality | manufacture |
| information | variety | detection | paragraph | telephone |

Now try these

1. Match the words on the scroll to their root word in the list below. Write down the pairs.

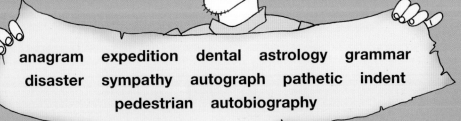

anagram   expedition   dental   astrology   grammar

disaster   sympathy   autograph   pathetic   indent

pedestrian   autobiography

a) **auto** (from Greek, meaning *self*)   b) **pathos** (from Greek, meaning *feeling*)

c) **gramma** (from Greek, meaning *written*)   d) **aster** (from Latin, meaning *star*)

e) **pedis** (from Latin, meaning *foot*)   f) **dentis** (from Latin, meaning *tooth*)

2.

Think of some more words with the same root word as the pairs above.

Using a dictionary

You can use a **dictionary** for finding the **meanings** of **words** and **checking** their **spelling**.

Guide words tell you the first and last word on the page.

Plurals are given.

This word has more than one meaning.

bunch   **buy**

bunch bunches (n.) A bunch is a group of things together.

burgle burgles burgling burgled (vb.) If you burgle a property you break in and steal things. burglar (n.) burglary (n.)

business businesses
1 (n.) A business is a place of work.
2 (n.) Your business consists of matters which concern you only.

busy busier busiest (adj.) If you are busy you have a lot of things to do.

buy buys buying bought (vb.) When you buy something you get it by paying for it.

"n." stands for noun, "adj." for adjective and "vb." for verb.

Additional linked words are given.

Different forms of the verb are given.

Practice

Write your answers using the page of the dictionary above.

1. The first word on the page is _____ and the last word is _____.

2. The words are arranged in a_____ o_____.

3. Write whether these words are nouns, verbs or adjectives:
   a) burgle   b) busy   c) buy
   d) bunch   e) burglary

4. Which word means to have a lot of things to do?

5. What's the plural of:
   a) bunch?   b) business?

More to think about

1. Write each set of words in alphabetical order.

   a) several   season   sewer   sequence   settle

   b) petal   pillar   pest   pill   pink

   c) cargo   caravan   caribou   cartoon   carpenter

   d) confess   consent   conduct   conceal   cone

2. These words are spelled incorrectly.
   Check them in a dictionary and then write them correctly.

   a) definate (certain)

   b) forain (from another country)

   c) seperate (apart)

   d) neihbour (someone next to you)

   e) exiteing (thrilling)

   f) proffesor (a teacher at a university)

   g) goverment (those who govern)

   h) pecooliar (strange)

Now try these

Use your dictionary to help you with the following questions.

1. Write a definition for each of these words.

   a) an album   b) a biography

   c) a directory   d) a register

2. Write down who or what would live in
   these places.

   a) a monastery   b) barracks

   c) an eyrie   d) an aviary

3. Write the difference between the words
   in each pair.

   a) root, route   b) bough, bow

   c) cereal, serial   d) sow, sew

4. Write two different meanings for these words.

   a) bulb   b) capsule

   c) lock   d) drive

Unit 6 Onomatopoeia

Onomatopoeia is when the **sound** of the word is **similar** to the **sound of the thing it describes**.

Have fun reading this rhyme. It has many onomatopoeic words in it.

What some people do

Jibber, jabber, gabble, babble,
Cackle, clack and prate,
Twiddle, twaddle, mutter, stutter,
Utter, splutter, blate …

Chatter, patter, tattle, prattle,
Chew the rag and crack,
Spiel and spout and spit it out,
Tell the world and quack …

Sniffle, snuffle, drawl and bawl,
Snicker, snort and snap,
Bark and buzz and yap and yelp,
Chin and chirp and chat …

Shout and shoot, gargle and gasp,
Gab and gag and groan,
Hem and haw and work the jaw,
Grumble, mumble, moan …

Beef and bellyache and bat,
Say a mouthful, squawk,
That is what some people do
When they merely talk.

Anonymous

Practice

Write down which animals these sounds remind you of.

1. Quack!

2. Woof!

3. Buzz! Buzz!

4. Baa!

5. Miaow!

6. Gobble! Gobble!

7. Hiss!

8. Neigh!

9. Toowit! Toowoo!

More to think about

Write down what these sets of onomatopoeic words remind you of.

1. plip-plop, pitter-patter, splish-splash

2. stomp, trample, crunch

3. whoosh, zoom, roar

4. hiss, slither, slide

5. squish, squash, squelch

6. Pow! Zap! Thwaapp!

7. screech, groan, moan

8. Rat-a-tat! Knock-knock! Ring-ring!

Now try these

1. Write down four onomatopoeic words to describe each of these. Make up your own if you like!

   a) the way different animals move

   b) the sounds of different insects

   c) the sounds of the wind

   d) kitchen sounds

2. Now try making up your own onomatopoem, like the one below, which tells a story through sound words only.

   Choose one of these titles:

   • "The Woods at Night"

   • "A Storm at Sea"

   • "The Building Site"

   or make up your own.

The Spooky House

Creep, creep, creep.
C R E A K!
Shhh! Husssh!
Tip-toe, tip-tap.
THUD! MOAN!
Grooaann!
Rittle-rattle.
SCREECH!
SMASH! CRASH!
Tiptaptiptaptiptap
Pant! Pant!
ZOOM!

Common expressions

In our everyday lives we use many **common expressions** or **sayings**.
Sometimes these sayings may be a little hard to understand!

All's well that ends well.

The saying "It's raining cats and dogs"
really means it's raining hard.

Practice

1. Match the sayings in the box to the pictures below. Write down the matching pairs.

> beat about the bush   have a bee in your bonnet   under a cloud
> let the cat out of the bag   take the bull by the horns   give up the ghost

a)

b)

c)

d)

e)

f)

2. Choose two sayings from Question 1. Write what you think they really mean.

More to think about

Copy these sayings. Use the correct word from the box
to complete each sentence.

chickens   brave   fire   absence   job   waste   noise   more

1. _____ makes the heart grow fonder.

2. To put on a _____ face.

3. Empty vessels make most _____.

4. The _____ the merrier.

5. Out of the frying pan into the _____.

6. _____ not, want not.

7. When a _____ is worth doing, it's worth doing well.

8. Don't count your _____ before they're hatched.

Now try these

Copy these sets of sayings and their meanings. Join the saying to its correct
meaning with a line.

to be a wet blanket	to refuse to take sides in an argument
to put the cart before the horse	to make little difficulties seem enormous
to sit on the fence	to be a spoilsport
to hang your head	to act while conditions are favourable
to strike while the iron is hot	to take punishment without complaint
to turn over a new leaf	to do things the wrong way round
to make a mountain out of a molehill	to get into trouble
to face the music	to be suspicious
to smell a rat	to make a fresh start
to get into hot water	to be ashamed of yourself

Figures of speech: similes and metaphors

A **figure of speech** is when you use words in a special way to create a **new or unusual meaning**.

Similes and metaphors use figurative language.

A **simile** is when one thing is compared to another by using the words **as** or **like**.

Cat is **as** quick **as** a flash of lightning.

When my Dad gets angry he's **like** a bull in a china shop.

A **metaphor** is when you describe something **as if it were something else**.

The digger was a dinosaur with a huge, gaping mouth and sharp teeth.

The wind is a giant's hand, pushing and snatching.

Practice

Copy the beginnings and endings of these well-known similes. Then match them together.

as sly as a	bat		as flat as a	cucumber
as blind as a	eel		as hard as	lead
as brave as a	bee		as heavy as	iron
as busy as a	fox		as light as a	pancake
as slippery as an	lion		as cool as a	feather

More to think about

Match each phrase with an appropriate metaphor.

> a skyscraper at night   a vacuum cleaner
> a foggy day   a cat screeching   an aeroplane
> a tree   a goldfish swimming   a banana

1. a giant with a thousand eyes

2. an iron bird

3. a yellow boomerang

4. a wheel that needs oiling

5. an old man's white beard

6. an amber traffic light in the rain

7. a green hand reaching for the sky

8. an angry monster sucking and roaring

1. Make up some of your own similes.
   Copy and complete these similes using your own words.

   a) My hair is _____.

   b) A letter box is _____.

   c) A hedgehog is _____.

2. What could be described as:

   a) flat as a pancake?

   b) heavy as lead?

   c) light as a feather?

3. These riddles are metaphors.
   Can you answer them?

   a) I am an elephant's head.
      I squirt water on the flowers with my trunk.

   b) I give off light, but I'm not a lamp.
      I melt, but I'm not a lolly.
      I disappear when you use me.

   c) What being goes on four legs in the morning,
      Two legs in the afternoon,
      And three legs in the evening?

Homophones

Homophones are words that **sound the same** but are **spelled differently** and have **different meanings**.

Aman **rowed** past a man who **rode** his horse on the side of the **road**.

Practice

1. Copy the sentences. Choose the correct homophone to complete each one.

   a) The (bow/bough) of the tree hung low under the weight of the snow.

   b) Susie wasn't sure (witch/which) was her jumper.

   c) There was a (creak/creek) as the door swung open.

   d) The (hare/hair) ran across the field.

   e) The tired travellers were pleased to see the (in/inn) where they could stop for the night.

   f) The (whole/hole) family were looking forward to their summer holiday.

2. Copy the homophones that weren't used in Question 1 and write a sentence using each one.

More to think about

1. Copy the sentences. Choose the correct homophone from the box to complete each sentence.

> there   their   they're

a) _____ going to bed in half an hour.

b) _____ are the keys we've been looking for!

c) Have you got _____ telephone number?

d) _____ going to get in trouble if they do that!

e) _____ dog fell off the boat and was soaked.

f) At the fair _____ were lots of exciting rides.

g) David and Louise were going to _____ Nan's house for Christmas.

2. Write a sentence using each word in the box above.

Now try these

Copy the words. Write a homophone to match each word.

1. weight	**2.** weather	**3.** meet
4. four	**5.** new	**6.** prey
7. pale	**8.** rain	**9.** sleigh
10. two	**11.** blue	**12.** fair

Borrowed words

English is a **living language**. Over the years we've **borrowed** many words from the languages of **other countries**.

These words are borrowed from different languages.

pizza
Italy

sketch
the Netherlands

jungle
India

moccasins
America

vase
France

boomerang
Australia

shawl
the Middle East

wok
China

Practice

Here are some words we've borrowed from the Netherlands.

deck	dock	easel	smuggle	skipper
sketch	schooner	yacht	landscape	hoist

1. Many Dutch people are great sailors. Write the words from the box that are connected with the sea or ships.

2. There have been many great Dutch artists. Write the words from the box that are connected with painting.

3. Write the words from the box containing:
   a) ck   b) sk   c) ch

24

More to think about

Here are some words we've borrowed from Italy.

spaghetti	pizza	volcano	piano	ravioli	opera
umbrella	confetti	pasta	studio	macaroni	solo

1. Many Italians love food! Write the words from the box that are connected with food.

2. Many Italians love music. Write the words from the box that are connected with music.

3. Write the words from the box that:

   a) end with **a**

   b) end with **i**

   c) end with **o**

   d) contain a double consonant.

Now try these

Here are some words borrowed from other countries.

caravan restaurant bungalow toboggan boomerang shampoo banquet boutique blizzard moose cotton ballet zero pyjamas cafe kangaroo

Key:
- Middle East
- India
- America
- Australia
- France

1. Copy the countries in the key. Write the words next to the country that each one came from.

2. Choose two words from each country. Write a sentence using each word to show you know the meaning of the word.

Using a thesaurus

A **thesaurus** is a book that contains sets of words (synonyms) grouped according to their meanings. **Synonyms** are words that have **similar meanings**. A thesaurus is arranged in **alphabetical order**.

main word | type of word | synonyms

I'm going to call for the doctor!

call	*v.*	name, send for, phone, shout
calm	*n.*	composure
	v.	quiet, pacify
	adj.	placid, unastonished
carry	*v.*	bring, take
catch	*v.*	capture, hear, seize
cave	*n.*	cavern
	v.	collapse, sink
change	*n.*	cash
	v.	adjust, alter, exchange, reorganise, switch, turn
clear	*v.*	empty
	adj.	empty, simple, transparent
clever	*adj.*	bright, cunning, skilful

adj. = adjective
n. = noun
v. = verb

Practice

1. Answer these questions using the thesaurus page above. Write down your answers.

   a) Which alternative words could be used for "clear"?

   b) List the words that are nouns.

   c) What type of word is the word "pacify".

   d) What's the word "seize" a synonym for?

   e) Write another synonym for the word "carry".

2. Write two words that would be listed after the word "clever" in this thesaurus. Write two synonyms for each word.

More to think about

1. Copy and complete the table below using your own words.

2. Add two further words with their synonyms to the table. Remember the words need to be in alphabetical order.

Word	Type of word	Synonyms
shut		
slide		
slowly		
small		
smooth		
soft		

Now try these

1. Look these words up in a thesaurus. Write the synonyms listed for each word.

   a) hard   b) picture   c) strong   d) mean

   e) angry   f) careless   g) test   h) show

2. Now use a thesaurus to help you list as many describing words as you can for each of these.

   a) a forest – green, muddy

   b) a classroom

   c) a frozen lake

   d) a hot day

   e) a plate of fruit

   f) some disruptive children

   g) a stormy sea

   h) a party

Dialect words

In **different areas** of the country some people have **different ways of saying the same things**. This use of words or grammar is called a **dialect**.

A dialect is different from an **accent**, which is to do with the **way we pronounce words**.

This is how some people in different areas might say, "He's just a small boy".

He's just a we'an.

Scotland

He's just a nipper.

London

He's just a lad.

Lancashire

Practice

1. Copy this verse from a poem that uses a Caribbean English dialect.

> Barry get a big bag,
> Barry climb de gate,
> Barry granny call 'im,
> But Barry couldn' wait.
> Im wan' get ova dere, bwoy,
> Before it get too late.

2. Copy the same verse in Standard English. Put the lines in the correct order.

> Barry's granny called him,
> Before it got too late.
> Barry climbed the gate,
> He wanted to get over there, boy,
> Barry got a big bag,
> But Barry couldn't wait.

More to think about

1. Many Cockneys in London talk in a dialect called rhyming slang. Match the words with their meanings and write them out.

I'm just calling my trouble and strife on the dog and bone.

a)
dog and bone	wife
apples and pears	head
plates of meat	telephone
trouble and strife	feet
skin and blister	teeth
lump of lead	hair
Barnet Fair	sister
Hampstead Heath	stairs

b)
mince pies	road
Cain and Abel	boots
frog and toad	money
sugar and honey	knees
round the houses	eyes
bread and cheese	tea
daisy roots	table
Rosie Lee	trousers

2. Make up six sentences containing some words in rhyming slang.

Now try these

Build your own dialect dictionary.
Copy these words and their meanings as a starting point.

Dialect word	Meaning
aye	yes
baffies	slippers
bairn	small child
banger	old car
daps	plimsolls
fainites	truce – "I give up"
mardy	spoilt
scarper	run away
scoff	eat
tatties	potatoes
wee	little

To start with, think of words that mean good or bad. There are often lots of dialect words to do with children, the weather, transport and food.

Progress Unit

1. Write a synonym to match each word.
   a) wide   b) large   c) warm   d) worried
   e) hit   f) tiny   g) fasten   h) shout

2. Write the abbreviations of these words.
   a) British Airways   b) United Kingdom
   c) World Wildlife Fund   d) miles per hour
   e) Mister   f) Member of Parliament

3. Copy the sentences. Use a different adverb
   to fill each gap.
   a) "Catch the ball," Ben called _____.
   b) "This soup has a fly in it," complained Mr Thomas _____.
   c) "Are you awake?" whispered Tessa _____.
   d) "Stop the dog barking!" Mum shouted _____.

4. Copy these words.
   Underline the root word that each comes from.
   Add another word that uses the same root word.
   a) inform   b) autograph   c) uncover
   d) television   e) colourful   f) disappear

5. Write each set of words in alphabetical order.
   a) knight   key   knock   kilometre
   b) regular   register   refuse   regret
   c) workshop   woodworm   wound   wing
   d) gravity   grass   grapefruit   grave
   e) alarm   air   allotment   album

6. Write some onomatopoeic words that represent:

   a) a horse walking down a road

   b) a clock

   c) a chicken

   d) leaves blowing in the wind.

7. Write the meaning of these common expressions.

   a) Waste not, want not.

   b) When a job's worth doing, it's worth doing well.

   c) Absence makes the heart grow fonder.

   d) To put on a brave face.

8. Copy these sentences. Circle the metaphors and underline the similes.

   a) When the lights went out Tuhil felt as blind as a bat.

   b) The snow was like a blanket covering the ground.

   c) The iron bird flew high in the sky.

   d) Dad slept as deeply as a hedgehog in hibernation.

   e) The hairdresser didn't know where to start on the wet mop.

9. Write a homophone for each word and then put each homophone in a sentence.

   a) whether   b) two   c) slay

10. All these words are borrowed from Italy. Copy the words and complete with a final letter.
What do you notice about all the final letters?

a)

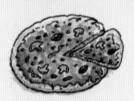

pizz__

b)

spaghett__

c)

pian__

d)

volcan__

e)

umbrell__

f)

oper__

11. Write a word you might find in a thesaurus that's linked to these synonyms.

   a) amusing, humorous, strange
   b) glum, tragic, unhappy
   c) batch, bundle, set
   d) faint, flimsy, feeble

12. Match each dialect word with its meaning.

| little   old car   plimsolls   eat   yes   potatoes |

   a) daps
   b) tatties
   c) wee
   d) aye
   e) scoff
   f) banger